THE
BORED
BOOK

WORD GAMES, QUIZZES, AND OTHER PHONE-FREE ACTIVITIES TO LIVEN UP YOUR DULL MOMENTS

This book combats the boredom of

_____

Ink & Willow

An Ink & Willow Trade Paperback Original

Copyright © 2024 by Penguin Random House LLC

Published in the United States by Ink & Willow, an imprint of Random House, a division of Penguin Random House LLC.

INK & WILLOW and colophon are registered trademarks of Penguin Random House LLC.

Interior illustrations: @ Sabrina Luoni: animal illustrations (pages 11, 43, 61, 77, 95). shutterstock.com: **HardtIllustrations,** marbled pattern (page 1); **Barks,** checkered pattern (pages 6–7, 96–97, 154–55); **bakhuj,** infinity sign (pages 10, 42, 76, 94); **Bagel Studio,** travel icons (pages 20, 72, 84, 142); **19srb81,** confidential stamp (pages 22, 40, 56, 74); **Pyty,** map (pages 26–27); **Callahan,** lettering (pages 38, 54, 73, 91, 114); **bardockstudio,** map (pages 68–69); **ExpressVectors,** pattern (pages 16, 34, 70, 113); **Vector Tradition,** paper (pages 137, 139)

Trade Paperback ISBN 978-0-593-58215-2

Printed in Malaysia

inkandwillow.com

9 8 7 6 5 4 3 2 1

Book and cover design by Danielle Deschenes
Cover art: shutterstock.com: **lukpedclub,** hand on book

Most Ink & Willow books are available at special quantity discounts for bulk purchase for premiums, fundraising, and corporate and educational needs by organizations, churches, and businesses. Special books or book excerpts also can be created to fit specific needs. For details, contact specialmarketscms@penguinrandomhouse.com.

CONTENTS

HOW NOT TO BE BORED
— 4 —

SOLO ACTIVITIES
— 7 —

MULTIPLAYER GAMES
97

ADVENTURES IN BEATING BOREDOM
— 155 —

-HOW-
NOT TO BE
BORED

People say nothing
is impossible,
BUT I DO NOTHING
EVERY DAY.

—A. A. MILNE

INTRODUCTIONS CAN BE REALLY BORING. And if you picked up this book, you're likely bored already, so let's keep this short, sweet, and maybe even a little interesting.

By the way, did you know that a sloth can slow down its heart rate and hold its breath underwater longer than a dolphin can? (See what we did there? Just trying to keep you on your toes.)

But back to the point.

THE PROBLEM

Boredom is an epidemic. According to one study, 63 percent of adults in the United States report feeling bored at least once every ten days.[1] Furthermore, over 60 percent of adults experience boredom weekly.[2] On average, American adults rack up as many as 131 "bored" days in any given year.[3]

To combat boredom, many people in recent years have been turning to what's easiest and most convenient, which usually ends up being the phone in their hand. In fact, many people—even when they don't actually feel bored—will turn to their phone just because it's "right there" and supposedly good at providing distraction. Though they might deny boredom, the symptom is the same: They need some kind of stimulation, so they grab what's handiest.

At the time of this book's publication, more than 91 percent of the global population owns a phone, and 86 percent of people have a smartphone.[4] Of those phone users, the average person tends to unlock their phone between 96 and 150 times a day (so once every ten minutes), checks their device within an hour of going to sleep and within five minutes of waking up, and may even spend more time looking at an electronic device than sleeping. If that doesn't sound like its own kind of epidemic of addiction, consider that as many as one-third of phone users surveyed across the globe admitted how challenging they find it to go on a technology break, even for a short time.[5]

And at this point, all of these statistics are probably much higher.

In other words, people are using their phones more and more and even getting addicted to them, but boredom isn't going away. On a more concerning note, our mental health appears to be declining year after year.[6] So if technology isn't helping, what other cures for boredom do we have at our fingertips?

So glad you asked! (And don't worry. Even though you're bored, we promise not to assign you any house chores just to give you something to do.)

THE SOLUTION

In a recent survey, studies found that boredom often results from a lack of "play" outlets, especially of the nostalgic variety.[7] (This will be great news for any adult who still enjoys Legos.) Basically, boredom rears its head when we haven't experienced enough play stimulation, and no amount of scrolling is going to scratch that playground itch in our souls. Which means, to beat boredom, we should return to our childhoods and schedule some game-focused playtime.

HOW TO USE THIS BOOK

When it comes to games and mindless fun, this little activity book is your one-stop shop. Divided into two main sections—Solo Activities and Multiplayer Games—The Bored Book offers mental stimulation for any boredom crisis that may pop up during your day.

If boredom strikes while you're by yourself or not in the mood to be around other people, turn to the Solo Activities section, where you'll find a wealth of "introvert" exercises such as word searches, coloring pages, thought therapy prompts, and more. If boredom hits you while you're with friends or feeling more extroverted, check out the Multiplayer Games section, which has a range of activities for two or more people, including tic-tac-toe, dots and boxes, and conversation starters. Throughout both sections, you will come across bonus "just for fun" pages that range from breath prayers and Scripture memory to jokes and random trivia. (Because sometimes all you need to break the cycle of boredom is a corny dad joke.)

At the end of this book is the Adventures in Beating Boredom section. On those pages, you can track your boredom journey, recognize when you're most susceptible to boredom, and even record your wins.

We would never wish boredom on anyone, but if you find yourself falling prey to it, may this book be your antidote. As you fill the pages, you'll become part of a new epidemic: one in which you're not bored of boredom but rather bored no more.

If we allow our "high creativity" to remain alive, we will never be bored. We can pray, standing in line at the super market. Or we can be lost in awe at all the people around us, their lives full of glory and tragedy, and suddenly we will have the beginnings of a painting, a story, a song.

—MADELEINE L'ENGLE

SOLO
ACTIVITIES

FOR ALL THOSE MOMENTS OF BOREDOM WHEN you're by yourself or not quite up to being chatty, redeem the time with one of the solo activities in this section. Whether you're hoping to fill two minutes or two hours, challenge yourself to be creative, dig deep, and make the most of the gift of time!

When riding in a car for more than six hours, you like to:

- **A)** read a book
- **B)** listen to music or a podcast
- **C)** start a game with your fellow travelers
- **D)** take a nap

You're sitting in a waiting room, and to kill time, you:

- **A)** flip through a magazine or book
- **B)** scroll through social media
- **C)** strike up a conversation with the person next to you
- **D)** zone out

While waiting for your meal to arrive at a restaurant, you:

- **A)** scan the menu again
- **B)** catch up on your text messages
- **C)** chat with the people at your table
- **D)** people watch

You're stuck waiting between classes or work meetings, so you:

- **A)** review any notes or organize your calendar
- **B)** check email
- **C)** talk to whoever else is waiting for the class or meeting to start
- **D)** find a corner to take a quick catnap in

You end up having a night at home with no plans. You:

- **A)** finish that book you've been dying to read all week
- **B)** catch up on your favorite show
- **C)** invite a friend to come hang out
- **D)** take a bubble bath and go to bed early

You should be working or finishing a project, but instead you:

- **A)** sneak a few more pages of your current read
- **B)** watch YouTube or TikTok videos
- **C)** share the latest celebrity news with your co-workers or deskmates
- **D)** do some yoga or meditation exercises

Your plane is delayed by four hours, and you're stuck in the airport. You:

- **A)** browse an airport bookstore for a new read or crossword puzzle
- **B)** watch one of those movies you downloaded
- **C)** wander to a different terminal and look for food
- **D)** stretch out at an empty gate and take a nap

You had to arrive early to claim your seat or spot in line for an event, but now you must wait several hours for the show to start. You:

- **A)** pull out the snacks you brought
- **B)** play games on your phone
- **C)** become friends with the people near you
- **D)** quietly make up stories about the people around you

The cashier line is especially long and slow. You:

- A) scan through the magazines on the rack
- B) pull out your phone to check email or social media
- C) start up small talk with the person in front of or behind you
- D) avoid the line and make an online delivery order

When you're outside for a walk or a run, you almost always:

- A) use the time to think through a project, problem, or recent conversation
- B) listen to an audiobook
- C) say hello to everyone you pass
- D) just enjoy the silence and scenery

SCORING

Mostly A's
BORED PREPPER

Boredom rarely sneaks up on you, and when it does, you're prepared, either with a book or an activity close at hand. Overall, you don't often sit still for long periods of time, unless you're getting something done or losing yourself in a great read. Just remember that you don't always have to "be productive." You can treat any in-between moments as an invitation to rest and enjoy a much-needed break. *[Challenge yourself by doing one of the Breath Prayers!]*

Mostly B's
BORED GAMER

Thanks to your mobile device, which is never far away, you're always able to immediately crush any hint of boredom that might peek its nose in your vicinity. Whether with games, streamed entertainment, or scrolling, you're never without something to do in any situation. Just be sure to look up every once in a while so you don't miss those priceless gems that might come from unexpected face-to-face interaction. *[Challenge yourself by completing one of the Visual Scavenger Hunts!]*

Mostly C's
BORED CONVERSER

You can't even remember the last time you were bored, mostly because you can always find something to do—or better yet, someone to talk to. Awkward pauses or long silences are definitely not your forte, and you tend to fill any you stumble into with friendly small talk or maybe even a fun conversation starter. Your peppy energy often provides a welcoming space for others, but just remember that quiet times are okay too and are sometimes even preferred by those around you. *[Challenge yourself by filling out one of the Thought Therapy pages!]*

Mostly D's
BORED LEISURER

If sleeping were a superpower, you could one day save the world. No one needs to remind you about the benefits of rest. After all, you're a champion at taking advantage of even the shortest breaks by catching quick catnaps—no matter where you are. You're also highly imaginative when you put your mind to it. Just remember to take the occasional break from people watching and get in on the action yourself sometimes. *[Challenge yourself by creating a Story Bored with another person!]*

Whether you're anxious, stressed, or just plain bored, try this breath prayer and allow the truth of the words to wash over you and fill you with peace. For each breath, inhale through your nose for four to five seconds, and then exhale through your mouth for four to five seconds, all while meditating on the phrases below.

(INHALE)

Be still and know

BREATH PRAYER

(EXHALE)

that He is God.

SHADING BY NUMBERS

1 2 3 4

HINT: Start with lighter shading. You can always go darker if you need to!

SCRIBBLY
SKETCHES

When boredom strikes, what better way to muddle through it than with sketching, doodling, and creating!

THOUGHT THERAPY

What are you looking forward to right now?

When was the last time you felt rested, and how can you experience that rest again?

What are you dreading or feeling anxious about?

When was the last time you felt incandescently happy, and what caused it?

DID YOU KNOW . . .

Movie trailers used to be viewed after the movie, which is how they earned the name "trailers."[1]

People from all social classes in medieval England would exchange insults by engaging in *flyting*, which was basically an early form of rap battle.[2]

During the Great Depression, many people began to make clothes out of the burlap sacks used to deliver food. As a result, the distribution companies started adding more color to the food bags for the sake of fashion.[3]

King Tut may have owned a dagger of extraterrestrial origin.[4]

Scotland's national animal is a unicorn.[5]

Harriet Tubman once carried chickens around with her as a disguise while helping slaves escape to freedom. When she saw her former master coming toward her, she released the chickens as a distraction and pretended she had to round them back up.[6]

ABOUT HISTORY?

THIS OR THAT

My Literary Style

○ reading	○ listening
○ fiction	○ nonfiction
○ bookstore	○ library
○ memoir	○ history
○ leave you hanging	○ wrapped up nicely
○ present tense	○ past tense
○ first-person narrator	○ third-person narrator
○ horror	○ suspense
○ Jane Austen	○ Emily Brontë
○ William Shakespeare	○ Charles Dickens
○ self-help	○ how-to
○ tragedy	○ comedy
○ poetry	○ prose
○ novel	○ comic
○ bookmarked	○ dog-eared
○ science fiction	○ fantasy
○ historical fiction	○ rom-com

INSPIRATION
STRIKES

Fill these pages with
your brilliant ideas,
designs, inventions,
or plans. (Sometimes
the best ideas come
during boredom.)

HELLO/ HI

LEARN THE LINGO

GOODBYE/ BYE

AFRIKAANS – Goeie dag / Hallo	**AFRIKAANS** – Totsiens / Mooi loop
ARABIC – مرحبا [Marhaba]	**ARABIC** – مع السلامة [Maʾ al-salāmah]
DUTCH – Hallo / Hoi	**DUTCH** – Dag / Tot ziens
ENGLISH – Hello / Hi	**ENGLISH** – Goodbye / Bye
FRENCH – Bonjour / Salut	**FRENCH** – Au revoir / Salut
GERMAN – Hallo / Hi	**GERMAN** – Auf Wiedersehen / Tschüss
HAWAIIAN – Aloha	**HAWAIIAN** – Aloha / A hui hou
HINDI – नमस्ते [Namaste]	**HINDI** – अलविदा [Alavida]
ITALIAN – Salve / Ciao	**ITALIAN** – Arrivederci / Ciao
JAPANESE – こんにちは [Konnichiwa]	**JAPANESE** – さようなら [Sayonara] / バイバイ [Bai-bai]
MANDARIN – 你好 [Nǐ hǎo]	**MANDARIN** – 再见 [Zàijiàn]
PORTUGUESE – Olá	**PORTUGUESE** – Adeus
RUSSIAN – Здравствуйте [Zdravstvuyte] / Привет [Privyet]	**RUSSIAN** – До свидания [Do svidaniya] / Пока [Poka]
SPANISH – Hola	**SPANISH** – Adiós
SWAHILI – Hujambo / Habari	**SWAHILI** – Kwaheri
UKRAINIAN – Добрий день [Dobri den]	**UKRAINIAN** – Бувай [Buvái]

VISUAL SCAVENGER

HUNT

— AT THE AIRPORT —

PERSON RUNNING TO CATCH A FLIGHT	SERVICE DOG	KID ON A LEASH	PERSON READING A NEWSPAPER
PERSON SLEEPING	PEOPLE PLAYING CARDS/ A GAME	FANCY CARRY-ON	SIGN FOR INTERNATIONAL CITY
SWEATSHIRT/ T-SHIRT WITH CITY NAME	SPORTS TEAM/ MISSION TEAM TRAVELERS	GRANDPARENTS	FAST-FOOD LINE WITH MORE THAN FIFTEEN PEOPLE
WEIRD ART	CELEBRITY	SOMEONE IGNORING "STAND RIGHT, WALK LEFT"	PERSON USING THE BORED BOOK

CHARACTER PROFILES

CONFIDENTIAL
TOP SECRET
CONFIDENTIAL

Choose a person nearby and create a fictional profile for them. Let your mind run wild with creativity, but remember to be kind! And if you come up with an epic character, write a story about them.

Person (woman reading book/man in red sweater/etc.):

Name:

Occupation:

Hometown:

Family of origin:

Currently waiting for: _____

Absolutely loves: _____
_____

Can't stand: _____
_____

On the way to: _____

Lifelong dream: _____
_____

Greatest passion: _____
_____

Annoyed at: _____
_____

Deepest fear: _____
_____

Darkest secret: _____
_____

SCRIPTURE

MEMORY

MATTHEW 5:1-12

Have a few extra minutes? Read through this passage and see how much of it you can memorize.

Now when Jesus saw the crowds, he went up on a mountainside and sat down. His disciples came to him, and he began to teach them.

He said:
"Blessed are the poor in spirit,
  for theirs is the kingdom of heaven.
Blessed are those who mourn,
  for they will be comforted.
Blessed are the meek,
  for they will inherit the earth.
Blessed are those who hunger and
  thirst for righteousness,
  for they will be filled.
Blessed are the merciful,
  for they will be shown mercy.
Blessed are the pure in heart,
  for they will see God.
Blessed are the peacemakers,
  for they will be called children
  of God.
Blessed are those who are persecuted
  because of righteousness,
  for theirs is the kingdom of heaven.

"Blessed are you when people insult you, persecute you and falsely say all kinds of evil against you because of me. Rejoice and be glad, because great is your reward in heaven, for in the same way they persecuted the prophets who were before you."

24

BORED WORD SEARCH

```
B E U N I N T E R E S T I N G
E O W O C X U V E G A I Y U E
Y G R J L V T S P L P I A A L
K E A E K O R K E P A T K Z B
I P R U D N W M T D T E I G A
Q Q S T N O S O I C H M D G N
B B A J E S M N T K Y D Z N I
W Z W P E D I O I S I D B I M
U V O L Q B I T O R I O T H R
P Y D T Q M L O N S R G V T E
F N U Q E P O N U I X Z H O T
E Q G X E I P Y N S E G L N N
Q K T X V K U G A C L O C K I
O J S Q J E F Q T K N C V B B
E C N E L I S E U G A Z T J Y
```

WORDS

APATHY

BOREDOM

BORING

CLOCK

ENDLESS

INTERMINABLE

LONG

MONOTONY

NOTHING

QUIET

REPETITION

SIGH

SILENCE

TEDIOUS

UNINTERESTING

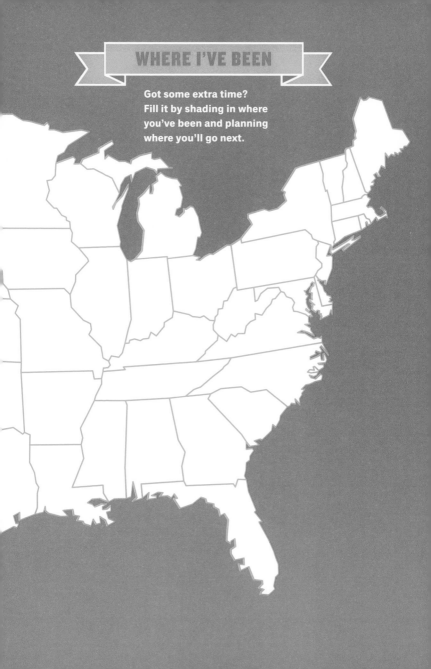

WHERE I'VE BEEN

Got some extra time?
Fill it by shading in where
you've been and planning
where you'll go next.

WHAT I LEARNED TODAY

Whether it is a revelation about yourself, a new software at work, the state of the world, or a useless trivia fact, you're always learning something. Jot down what you've learned recently in the space below.

29

GET IT DONE

- [ ]
- [ ]
- [ ]
- [ ]
- [ ]
- [ ]
- [ ]
- [ ]
- [ ]
- [ ]
- [ ]
- [ ]
- [ ]
- [ ]
- [ ]
- [ ]
- [ ]

Being bored and being productive rarely go hand in hand, so instead of feeling guilty the next time boredom strikes, simply write down what you have to do and leave it at that. You can check each task off your list later, but at least acknowledging each to-do item is taking a step in the right direction!

- [ ]
- [ ]
- [ ]
- [ ]
- [ ]
- [ ]
- [ ]
- [ ]
- [ ]
- [ ]
- [ ]
- [ ]
- [ ]
- [ ]
- [ ]
- [ ]
- [ ]

What Type of READER ARE YOU?*

Place a checkmark next to each item that describes you.

○ You often stay up late to finish a book—eating and sleeping are just inconveniences to what really matters in life!

○ Sometimes you're late to appointments because you need to finish the chapter you're on.

○ You watch every movie adaptation of your favorite books—and of course the book was better.

○ Your favorite pastime is browsing the shelves at your local bookstore.

○ You complete the book you're reading even if you're not loving it—gotta meet that Goodreads goal!

○ You always have a book with you so you can read whenever there's a free moment.

○ Your weekend plans always include curling up with a good book in your favorite reading spot.

○ You don't have a to-be-read pile—you have piles . . . upon piles upon piles.

○ During your nine-to-five, you often think about diving back into your current read as soon as you get home.

○ You spend hours organizing your bookshelf by color, author, or genre.

○ You own book-themed clothes, mugs, prints, and/or stickers.

○ You're truly sad when you finish a book, especially if it isn't part of a series— it's literally closing a chapter on part of your life.

○ You read or listen to an audiobook during your commute to work.

○ Part of your New Year's resolution is the number of books you plan to read.

○ You often start conversations with "What are you reading?"

○ Your friends consider you the go-to person for book recommendations—they know they can always trust you to introduce them to their latest favorite read.

○ You pack multiple books in your suitcase when traveling, even if you know you won't get to all of them. Can't hurt to have options!

○ You buy additional copies of your favorite book to make sure all your closest friends and family members also fall in love with it.

○ Every payday, you calculate how many books you can buy after rent, utilities, food, and all the other essentials are covered.

○ You equate free time with reading time— what else would you possibly be doing?

○ Your birthday and Christmas wish lists are made up almost entirely of books.

○ You often consider naming your future children or pets after your favorite authors and/or characters—if you haven't already.

○ When you make plans to socialize, you suggest hanging out in a bookstore, getting together for a book club, or attending a local author event.

○ You immediately text all your friends when your favorite author likes your Instagram post.

○ You don't mind when someone is running late for a get-together—that just means extra reading time!

○ After finishing a book, you often jump online to see what other readers thought of the ending—and if they didn't like it as much as you, they're obviously wrong!

○ You get excited when you wake up and realize you still have several chapters left in your current read.

○ You find yourself talking about characters as if they're actual people—and when others ask who they are, you sigh in disappointment before explaining.

○ After finishing a book, you immediately update your progress on Goodreads so you're closer to completing your annual reading challenge.

SCORING

REASONABLY BOOKISH: You love reading, but it hasn't taken over your life—yet. You're not afraid to admit that you love a good book or to make recommendations to your friends. However, you also value your sleep and your human friendships, so you make sure those are higher on your list of priorities.

UNDOUBTEDLY BOOKISH: No one would mistake you for a non-reader. You spend your free time at your local library or with your book club, and there's no hiding the stacks of books in your home when guests come over. You're proud to be a book nerd and love sharing the joy of reading with others.

TIME-FOR-AN-INTERVENTION BOOKISH: You live and breathe books. You wouldn't be caught dead without a good read in your backpack or purse, and you dream of a life that allows you to read books all day, every day. Sometimes your friends call to make sure you're still alive, and though you're reluctant to answer the phone, you assure them you're just immersed in your latest read.

---

* Originally published in Ink & Willow's *To Read or Not to Read: A Literary Journal for the Book Lover's Soul* (Colorado Springs: WaterBrook, 2020).

DID YOU KNOW . . .

One recycled tin can conserves enough energy to power a television for three hours.[7]

A peanut butter and jelly sandwich was a popular staple for soldiers during World War II.[8]

The most stolen food item in the world is cheese, with about 4 percent of all cheese produced being stolen.[9]

The candy bar called 3 Musketeers was originally invented with a three-part filling: chocolate, vanilla, and strawberry. But due to rationing during World War II, the gooey inside was simplified to chocolate only.[10]

Cucumbers are 95 percent water, cauliflowers are 92 percent, and strawberries are 91 percent.[11]

Since the words *hamburger* and *sauerkraut* sounded too German and therefore unpatriotic during World War II, Americans briefly renamed them "liberty steak" and "liberty cabbage," respectively.[12]

Honey is one of the only foods known to have an eternal shelf life, since it never goes bad.[13]

ABOUT FOOD?

THIS OR THAT

My Foodie Style

THIS	THAT
○ salty	○ sweet
○ spicy	○ mild
○ eating out	○ dining in
○ fast food	○ restaurant
○ inside	○ outside
○ food truck	○ picnic
○ sautéed	○ fried
○ chocolate	○ vanilla
○ cake	○ ice cream
○ meal prep	○ cafeteria
○ soup	○ salad
○ meat	○ vegetarian
○ stew	○ chili
○ pepperoni	○ Hawaiian
○ barbecue	○ charcuterie
○ chicken	○ fish
○ fruit	○ vegetable

INSPIRATION
STRIKES

Fill these pages with
your brilliant ideas,
designs, inventions,
or plans. (Sometimes
the best ideas come
during boredom.)

VISUAL SCAVENGER

HUNT

— IN THE CLASSROOM/OFFICE —

PERSON TAKING NOTES BY HAND	DIGITAL CLOCK	PERSON WEARING A TIE	CALCULATOR
PERSON FALLING ASLEEP	MECHANICAL PENCIL	HOLE PUNCH	FISH TANK
DESK FAN	SOMETHING YOU'VE NEVER NOTICED BEFORE	MOTIVATIONAL POSTER	SUCCULENT
GRAPHIC T-SHIRT	OLD-SCHOOL TECHNOLOGY	NAMEPLATE	COFFEE CUP

MINDFUL WORD SEARCH

```
N O E G R Z M M X W Q W D X H
Q Q E R W W K H O D T J R A T
M B I J A W B D N A F Y A W G
P R O D U C T I V E W R G A W
A E K W U Z L F M H G A E K E
M C G X K U C J O R C I R E L
W N A R F D A L Q N V S K E L
N E G D E Z E Z V H T C J O B
T D N Y N M E N T A L I T Y E
R I Y P P A H L B J Q W Q O I
M F L R D B A I W J Q Z Q C N
Z N Y Q B E L E C N A L A B G
D O M E H I F W T T R L U X R
B C Q X T C O N N E C T I O N
X M K Y I F C A H X Y Q F K T
```

WORDS

AWAKE
AWARE
BALANCE
CARE
CONFIDENCE
CONNECTION
HAPPY
HEALTH

MENTALITY
MINDFUL
PRODUCTIVE
REGARD
STABILITY
WELL-BEING
WHOLE

CHARACTER PROFILES

CONFIDENTIAL
TOP SECRET
CONFIDENTIAL

Choose a person nearby and create a fictional profile for them. Let your mind run wild with creativity, but remember to be kind! And if you come up with an epic character, write a story about them.

Person (woman reading book/man in red sweater/etc.):

Name:

Alias:

Nationality:

Criminal specialty:

Wanted for: _____

Latest crime: _____

Currently preparing for: _____
_____

First crime: _____
_____

Greatest skill: _____
_____

Hidden weakness: _____
_____

Weapon of choice: _____

Partner in crime: _____

Ultimate heist goal: _____
_____

Deepest secret: _____
_____

Whether you're anxious, stressed, or just plain bored, try this breath prayer and allow the truth of the words to wash over you and fill you with peace. For each breath, inhale through your nose for four to five seconds, and then exhale through your mouth for four to five seconds, all while meditating on the phrases below. Repeat five to seven times, or as much as needed.

(INHALE)

The Lord is my shepherd.

BREATH PRAYER

(EXHALE)

I don't need anything else.

SHADING BY NUMBERS

| 1 | 2 | 3 | 4 |

HINT: Start with lighter shading. You can always go darker if you need to!

THOUGHT THERAPY

Who has made a big difference in your life? How so?

If you could have a conversation with anyone in the world, alive or dead, who would it be and what would you talk about?

Whom do you know that needs encouragement today?
Write down what you would say to them.

Who always makes you laugh or feel better?
What do you admire about them?

GET IT DONE

Being bored and being productive rarely go hand in hand, so instead of feeling guilty the next time boredom strikes, simply write down what you have to do and leave it at that. You can check each task off your list later, but at least acknowledging each to-do item is taking a step in the right direction!

- [ ]
- [ ]
- [ ]
- [ ]
- [ ]
- [ ]
- [ ]
- [ ]
- [ ]
- [ ]
- [ ]
- [ ]
- [ ]
- [ ]
- [ ]
- [ ]
- [ ]

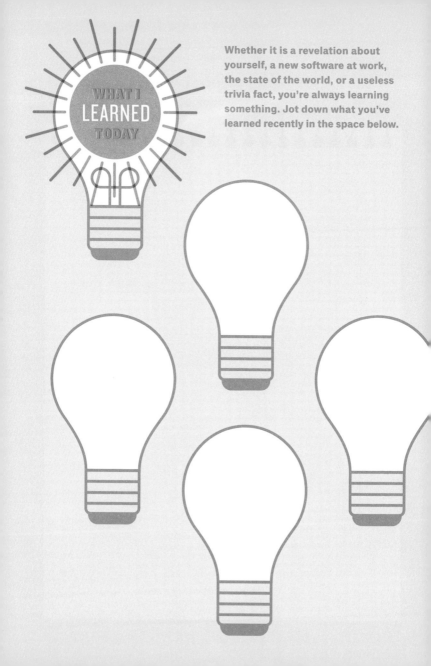

WHAT I LEARNED TODAY

Whether it is a revelation about yourself, a new software at work, the state of the world, or a useless trivia fact, you're always learning something. Jot down what you've learned recently in the space below.

SCRIBBLY SKETCHES

When boredom strikes, what better way to muddle through it than with sketching, doodling, and creating!

What's Your
TRAVEL STYLE?

**Place a checkmark next to each
item that describes you.**

○ You've traveled to all fifty states.

○ You make it a goal to travel internationally at least once a year.

○ You have been on an overnight backpacking or camping trip.

○ You have more than five stamps in your passport.

○ You've been on at least one cruise.

○ You like experiencing new cultures and cuisines.

○ You would consider yourself an experienced packer.

○ You got your passport before the age of eighteen.

○ You've visited at least ten countries.

○ You can have a basic conversation in another language.

○ You tend to plan your next vacation as soon as you get home from one.

○ You collect a specific souvenir from every place you travel.

○ You've traveled by plane, train, and boat.

○ You have sent a postcard from a vacation destination.

○ You have planned and executed at least one road trip.

○ You have been to at least three national parks.

○ You have gone on at least one spontaneous trip or vacation.

○ You've intentionally traveled to attend a festival, event, or concert.

○ You have stayed at an all-inclusive resort.

○ At some point, you have gone on vacation to the lake, the beach, the mountains, and a destination city.

○ You have a routine every time you go through an airport.

○ You've gone on at least two solo trips.

○ You have intentionally played "tourist" in your own city.

○ You have gone swimming in at least three different oceans.

○ You have at least one frequent flyer account or a hotel points membership.

○ You travel for at least one major holiday every year.

○ You have more than one type of foreign currency or stamp at your house.

○ You have booked at least one trip just because a cheap flight deal popped up.

○ You've traveled to all seven continents.

CASUAL VACATIONER: You like traveling—and you definitely have favorite vacation spots that you might have visited more than once—but you also recognize the value of being at home. And while you don't necessarily shy away from the occasional big trip, you tend to prioritize strengthening your hometown roots and cultivating strong relationships with those in your immediate circle.

FREQUENT FLYER: You live for your next vacation and love having at least one or two fun trips scheduled on your calendar every year. You may not always be up for those international excursions (we get it—traveling is expensive!), but you are definitely an avid explorer of your own country. Still, when those flight deals to far-off places do pop up, you're quick to grab them so you can fulfill your passion to experience something new.

PROFESSIONAL GLOBE-TROTTER: If traveling the world could be your full-time gig, you'd definitely quit your day job, which you really only have so you can support your travel habit. When you're not actively traveling, you're excitedly planning your next adventure, brushing up on your foreign language skills, or dreaming about all the places still on your bucket list. And while someone with as many passport stamps as you doesn't need travel tips, be sure you keep *The Bored Book* handy for that next unexpected layover.

VISUAL SCAVENGER

HUNT

— IN THE WAITING ROOM —

CLIPBOARD	POTTED PLANT	PERSON READING A BOOK	MAGAZINE
TV	PICTURE OF AN ANIMAL	CANDY	SOMETHING BROKEN
CLOCK	SOMEONE TALKING ON THE PHONE	CLOTHING LOGO	SOMETHING PURPLE
FANDOM PARAPHERNALIA	CALENDAR	NON-WHITE SHOELACE	WATER BOTTLE

THOUGHTFUL WORD SEARCH

```
T Y S V F Q C I Z Q U C S C K
Q H T S E R D O M S E L O N T
P W O I E O Z R N M N N X I M
E N B U L N E B W S T H Z A E
C B H C G L L E F E I V J R D
A L Z N A H K L M R V D X B I
E W T X U W T P I R L Y E L T
P T J U I X L S E T Z Q M R A
W Y C Y A A L D Q U S C G H T
A X F A T O N R E F L E C T I
T H Z I R O E Z Y L A N A D O
C T O K P T Q Y Y C D Q N O N
H N S K X Y S X Q A T I Y E E
H B O O O A O B N T M B T J B
W E Q K F K I C A X Q A V U W
```

WORDS

ABSTRACT	PEACE
ANALYZE	PONDER
BRAIN	REFLECT
CONSIDER	RELAX
CONTEMPLATION	REST
MEDITATION	STILLNESS
MIND	THOUGHTS
	WATCH

CHARACTER PROFILES

Choose a person nearby and create a fictional profile for them. Let your mind run wild with creativity, but remember to be kind! And if you come up with an epic character, write a story about them.

Person (woman reading book/man in red sweater/etc.):

Name:

Superhero name:

Superpower:

Hero or villain:

City of residence: _____

Known family: _____

_____

Latest superhero gig: _____

_____

Archnemesis: _____

Sidekick/ally: _____

Greatest strength: _____

_____

Greatest downfall: _____

_____

Origin story: _____

_____

_____

_____

_____

THOUGHT THERAPY

What is one of your happiest memories? Why?

What difficult or disappointing event in your life is still shaping you today? In what way?

What are you most looking forward to right now? Why?

What are you hoping to accomplish or achieve?

SCRIPTURE MEMORY

PHILIPPIANS 2:1-11, ESV

Have a few extra minutes? Read through this passage and see how much of it you can memorize.

If there is any encouragement in Christ, any comfort from love, any participation in the Spirit, any affection and sympathy, complete my joy by being of the same mind, having the same love, being in full accord and of one mind. Do nothing from selfish ambition or conceit, but in humility count others more significant than yourselves. Let each of you look not only to his own interests, but also to the interests of others. Have this mind among yourselves, which is yours in Christ Jesus, who, though he was in the form of God, did not count equality with God a thing to be grasped, but emptied himself, by taking the form of a servant, being born in the likeness of men. And being found in human form, he humbled himself by becoming obedient to the point of death, even death on a cross. Therefore God has highly exalted him and bestowed on him the name that is above every name, so that at the name of Jesus every knee should bow, in heaven and on earth and under the earth, and every tongue confess that Jesus Christ is Lord, to the glory of God the Father.

SHADING BY NUMBERS

1 2 3 4

HINT: Start with lighter shading. You can always go darker if you need to!

INSPIRATION
STRIKES

Fill these pages with
your brilliant ideas,
designs, inventions,
or plans. (Sometimes
the best ideas come
during boredom.)

GET IT DONE

- [ ]
- [ ]
- [ ]
- [ ]
- [ ]
- [ ]
- [ ]
- [ ]
- [ ]
- [ ]
- [ ]
- [ ]
- [ ]
- [ ]
- [ ]
- [ ]
- [ ]
- [ ]

Being bored and being productive rarely go hand in hand, so instead of feeling guilty the next time boredom strikes, simply write down what you have to do and leave it at that. You can check each task off your list later, but at least acknowledging each to-do item is taking a step in the right direction!

- [ ]
- [ ]
- [ ]
- [ ]
- [ ]
- [ ]
- [ ]
- [ ]
- [ ]
- [ ]
- [ ]
- [ ]
- [ ]
- [ ]
- [ ]
- [ ]
- [ ]

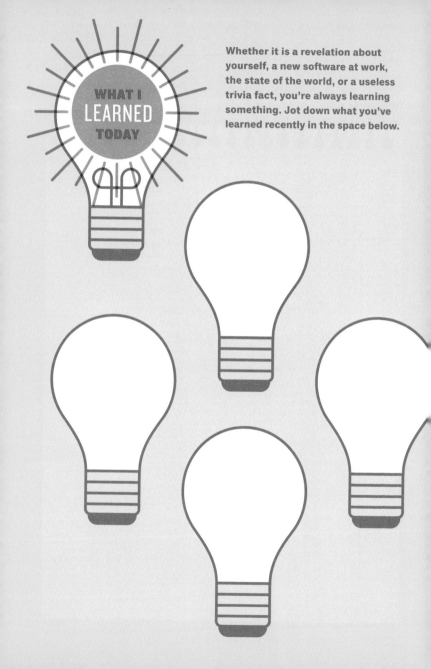

WHAT I LEARNED TODAY

Whether it is a revelation about yourself, a new software at work, the state of the world, or a useless trivia fact, you're always learning something. Jot down what you've learned recently in the space below.

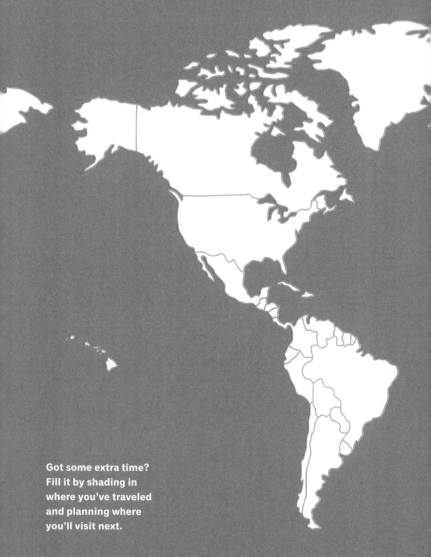

WHERE I'VE TRAVELED

Got some extra time?
Fill it by shading in
where you've traveled
and planning where
you'll visit next.

DID YOU KNOW . . .

In Japan, trains almost always run on time, but when there's even a five-minute delay, staff will hand out "delay certificates" to offer as proof to bosses or teachers.[14]

In Australia, you can visit a new beach every day for twenty-seven years and still not hit all ten thousand.[15]

Russia is bigger than Pluto.[16]

In Sweden, a popular pizza topping is sliced banana and curry powder.[17]

China has only one national time zone across the whole country, even though it spans five geographical time zones.[18]

Even though we consider space the final frontier, we still have about 95 percent of the ocean left to explore.[19]

Since the Aleutian Islands cross the 180th meridian, Alaska actually exists in both the Western and Eastern Hemispheres.[20]

Papua New Guinea is home to 12 percent of the world's languages, with over 820 being spoken there.[21]

ABOUT TRAVEL?

My Travel Style

○ car	○ plane
○ train	○ boat
○ beach	○ mountain
○ road trip	○ camping
○ packed lunch	○ drive-thru
○ staycation	○ whirlwind tour
○ plan ahead	○ plan as you go
○ city	○ wilderness
○ national park	○ theme park
○ museum	○ music festival
○ travel light	○ pack plenty
○ family vacation	○ friend adventure
○ podcast	○ music
○ AC	○ rolled-down windows
○ tour guide	○ self-guided
○ journey	○ destination
○ all-inclusive resort	○ choose your own adventure

HOW ARE YOU?

LEARN THE LINGO

GOOD/ BORED

AFRIKAANS – Hoe gaan dit met jou?	**AFRIKAANS** – Goed / Verveeld
ARABIC – ?كيف حالك [Kaïfa ḥaluka?]	**ARABIC** – بخير [Beḥeïr] / مصاب بالملل [Musab bialmalal]
DUTCH – Hoe gaat het?	**DUTCH** – Goed / Verveeld
ENGLISH – How are you?	**ENGLISH** – Good / Bored
FRENCH – Comment ça va?	**FRENCH** – Bien / Ennuyé[e]
GERMAN – Wie geht es Ihnen? / dir? (formal / informal)	**GERMAN** – Gut / Gelangweilt
HAWAIIAN – Pehea ʻoe?	**HAWAIIAN** – MaikaʻI / Manakā
HINDI – क्या हाल है? [Kya haal hai?]	**HINDI** – ठीक [Theek] / ऊबा हुआ [Ooba hua]
ITALIAN – Come sta? / stai? (formal / informal)	**ITALIAN** – Bene / Annoiato/a
JAPANESE – おげんきですか? [O genki desu ka?]	**JAPANESE** – 元気です [Genki desu] / 退屈 [Taikutsu]
MANDARIN – 你好吗? [Nǐ hǎo ma?]	**MANDARIN** – 很好 [Hěn hǎo] / 无聊 的 [Wúliáo de]
PORTUGUESE – Tudo bem? / Tudo bom?	**PORTUGUESE** – Bom / Bem / Entediado/a
RUSSIAN – Как дела? [Kak dela?]	**RUSSIAN** – Хорошо [Khorosho] / Скучающий [Skuchayushchiy]
SPANISH – ¿Cómo estás?	**SPANISH** – Bien / Aburrido/a
SWAHILI – Hujambo? / U hali gani?	**SWAHILI** – Nzuri / Njema / Choshwa
UKRAINIAN – Як справи? [Jak správy?]	**UKRAINIAN** – добре [Dobre] / нудно [Nudno]

VISUAL SCAVENGER

— ON THE ROAD —

WIND TURBINE	CONVERTIBLE	KIDS WATCHING A MOVIE IN THEIR CAR	DOG WITH HEAD OUT THE WINDOW
HORSE TRAILER	BRIDGE	RV	ROAD WORK AHEAD *SIGN*
MOTORCYCLE GANG	TRAFFIC CONE	TWIN CARS	CHURCH STEEPLE
FARM STAND	BIBLE BILLBOARD	JUST MARRIED SIGN	BABY ANIMAL

CHARACTER PROFILES

CONFIDENTIAL
TOP SECRET
CONFIDENTIAL

Choose a person nearby and create a fictional profile for them. Let your mind run wild with creativity, but remember to be kind! And if you come up with an epic character, write a story about them.

Person (woman reading book/man in red sweater/etc.):

Name:

Code name:

Nationality:

Spy mission: _____

_____

Undercover occupation: _____

Current target: _____

List of skills: _____

_____

List of assets: _____

_____

Languages spoken: _____

_____

Most likely to be awarded: _____

Secret nightmare: _____

_____

Recruited/volunteered because: _____

_____

_____

Whether you're anxious, stressed, or just plain bored, try this breath prayer and allow the truth of the words to wash over you and fill you with peace. For each breath, inhale through your nose for four to five seconds, and then exhale through your mouth for four to five seconds, all while meditating on the phrases below. Repeat five to seven times, or as much as needed.

(INHALE)

Have mercy on me, God.

BREATH PRAYER

(EXHALE)

Restore my soul.

SHADING BY NUMBERS

| 1 | 2 | 3 | 4 |

HINT: Start with lighter shading. You can always go darker if you need to!

THOUGHT THERAPY

What matters most to you or makes you feel alive?

What is a fear you have conquered or are still trying to work through?

When do you most feel like "you"?

What is something you're holding on to (a physical object, person, or unhealthy habit or emotion) that you would like to let go of? How will you go about doing that?

What Type of SPORTS FAN ARE YOU?

Place a checkmark next to each item that describes you.

- ○ You own at least one jersey (and have worn it in public!).
- ○ You've gone to at least five sporting events in the past year.
- ○ You know your team's starting lineup.
- ○ You've hosted a watch party to cheer on your team.
- ○ You've participated in fantasy leagues.
- ○ You regularly trash-talk at games, sporting events, or in everyday life.
- ○ You have played in an amateur sports league.
- ○ You watch at least one professional draft a year.
- ○ You have a superstitious ritual that you do every time your favorite team plays.
- ○ You've named a pet after your favorite team or player.
- ○ You've watched at least twenty sports films.
- ○ You've read a memoir or biography about your favorite player.
- ○ You own some form of signed memorabilia.
- ○ You have intentionally gone to meet a professional athlete.
- ○ You have coached a sport.
- ○ Your friends consider you the go-to person for any kind of sports updates.
- ○ You can name more than ten teams in multiple leagues.
- ○ You own season tickets for your local team's games.
- ○ You have tailgated at more than five sporting events.
- ○ When asked what five people you would want to have dinner with, you list at least one athlete.
- ○ You have a favorite (and least favorite) commentator.
- ○ You subscribe to some form of sports media (streaming, magazine, channel, etc.).
- ○ You follow your favorite athletes or teams on social media.
- ○ When talking about your team, you refer to them as "we."
- ○ You watch all-star weekends.
- ○ You have cried after a big win.
- ○ You often get into debates about why your team is the best.
- ○ You always get sports trivia correct.
- ○ You find an excuse to bring sports into any conversation, business meeting, or interaction with a stranger.

SCORING

≤10

HERE-FOR-THE-SNACKS SPORTS FAN: You tolerate sports because it usually means hanging out with friends and eating lots of yummy food. You may know how points are scored during a game but not necessarily which team plays for which city or even who the biggest player is right now. Those kinds of details are clearly not as important as what kind of appetizers will be at the next watch party. Because the game will just be on in the background, right?

11–20

MINOR LEAGUE SPORTS FAN: You are committed to at least one or two sports. For the sports you're not interested in, you won't waste time following them. But you love watching games at home or out with people. You may even have a jersey. You really come alive during playoffs, which you consider your time to shine. When it comes down to who will be the next champion— especially if your favorite team is in the running—you're watching every game.

21–29

HALL-OF-FAMER SPORTS FAN: You love your sports! You want to talk stats, GOATs, and game replays every chance you get, and you try to watch as many games as possible. Since you most likely grew up watching sports, you now have a long-standing loyalty to your team that only other Hall-of-Fame-level fans could understand. You collect sports movies, jerseys, and lucky hats, and you know what it means to cry over a game. In fact, few can understand better than you the excitement that comes from a game-winning shot, Hail Mary pass, or penalty shoot-out.

- [ ] Fill out this entire book
- [ ] Run a marathon
- [ ] Study a foreign language
- [ ] Bring cookies to a neighbor
- [ ] Travel on an overseas flight
- [ ] Learn to play chess
- [ ] Go on a cruise
- [ ] Finish a classic novel
- [ ] Go bungee jumping
- [ ] Learn to play an instrument
- [ ] Go backpacking/camping
- [ ] Visit all fifty states
- [ ] Volunteer at a mission organization
- [ ] Ride in a hot-air balloon
- [ ] Explore a cave
- [ ] Go scuba diving or snorkeling
- [ ] Participate in a drama or musical

- [ ] Summit a volcano
- [ ] Travel by bus or train
- [ ] Swim in a hot spring
- [ ] See a waterfall
- [ ] Try a new sport
- [ ] Go on a safari
- [ ] Visit a science/natural history museum
- [ ] Attend live theater
- [ ] Visit a national park
- [ ] Take a vacation with friends
- [ ] Plant a garden
- [ ] Accomplish a major goal
- [ ] Create a piece of art
- [ ] Meet a celebrity
- [ ] Attend a formal event
- [ ] Cook a fancy meal/dish
- [ ] See the northern lights

Got some extra time? Fill it by figuring out what unusual or crazy things you've done and what might be next on your list.

- [ ] Go on a swamp tour
- [ ] Attend a music festival
- [ ] Host an event
- [ ] Read the Bible in a year
- [ ] Go on a mission trip
- [ ] Learn how to drive stick shift
- [ ] Learn a new dance
- [ ] Take a self-defense class
- [ ] Put together a 1,000-piece puzzle
- [ ] Swim in an ocean
- [ ] Dance in the rain
- [ ] Join a book club
- [ ] Conquer a fear
- [ ] Learn CPR
- [ ] Unplug for a week
- [ ] Sponsor a child
- [ ] Teach a class

- [ ] Host a charcuterie party
- [ ] Stay at a resort
- [ ] Explore a new place
- [ ] Try a new food
- [ ] Whistle with two fingers
- [ ] Score a winning point
- [ ] Make a scrapbook/photo album
- [ ] Plan a vacation
- [ ] Restore a piece of furniture
- [ ] Flip a house
- [ ] Go roller-skating
- [ ] _____
- [ ] _____
- [ ] _____
- [ ] _____
- [ ] _____
- [ ] _____

THANK YOU

LEARN THE LINGO

YOU'RE WELCOME

AFRIKAANS – Dankie	**AFRIKAANS** – Jy is welkom / Dit is 'n plesier
ARABIC – شُكْرًا [Šukran]	**ARABIC** – عفوًا [Afwan]
DUTCH – Dank u wel / Bedankt	**DUTCH** – Graag gedaan
ENGLISH – Thank you	**ENGLISH** – You're welcome
FRENCH – Merci	**FRENCH** – De rien / Je vous en prie
GERMAN – Danke	**GERMAN** – Bitte
HAWAIIAN – Mahalo	**HAWAIIAN** – A'ole pilikia
HINDI – धन्यवाद [Dhanyavaad]	**HINDI** – कोई बात नहीं [Koii baat nahiin]
ITALIAN – Grazie	**ITALIAN** – Prego
JAPANESE – ありがとう [Arigatō]	**JAPANESE** – どういたしまして [Dō itashimashite]
MANDARIN – 谢谢 [Xiè xiè]	**MANDARIN** – 不用谢 [Bù yòng xiè]
PORTUGUESE – Obrigado/a	**PORTUGUESE** – De nada
RUSSIAN – Спасибо [Spaseeba]	**RUSSIAN** – Пожалуйста [Pahszhalsta]
SPANISH – Gracias	**SPANISH** – De nada
SWAHILI – Asante	**SWAHILI** – Hakuna shida / Karibu
UKRAINIAN – Дякую [Dyakuyu]	**UKRAINIAN** – Прошу [Proshu]

CREATIVE WORD SEARCH

```
P J A H J R F E W A G F W L E
X S O X M W A K K U V O X B I
Q P L A M W N W W O N D E R R
E T G R Q D T O H J A L V X E
S I M M Y X A O M I W P X W V
C A O J O E S Y X M M Q B R E
A P G M T A Y H S I W S Q B R
P W Y A L C L N D M F B Y T X
E J E T K Z O D W Y A X Y A E
F R U A U I F I R Z H T I S N
C G T Y S A U N Y E B X K P I
B E L I E V E R D A A I B V G
O D V B V A Y B P D V M Q A A
U Y J T Q Q S O I P I Q E W M
W X Z M T W F L B Y J L P H I
```

WORDS

AWE	IMAGINE
BEAUTY	MAGIC
BELIEVE	REVERIE
CREATE	VISION
DREAM	WHIMSY
ESCAPE	WISH
FANTASY	WONDER
HOPE	

WHAT I LEARNED TODAY

Whether it is a revelation about yourself, a new software at work, the state of the world, or a useless trivia fact, you're always learning something. Jot down what you've learned recently in the space below.

GET IT DONE

- [ ]
- [ ]
- [ ]
- [ ]
- [ ]
- [ ]
- [ ]
- [ ]
- [ ]
- [ ]
- [ ]
- [ ]
- [ ]
- [ ]
- [ ]
- [ ]
- [ ]

Being bored and being productive rarely go hand in hand, so instead of feeling guilty the next time boredom strikes, simply write down what you have to do and leave it at that. You can check each task off your list later, but at least acknowledging each to-do item is taking a step in the right direction!

- [ ]
- [ ]
- [ ]
- [ ]
- [ ]
- [ ]
- [ ]
- [ ]
- [ ]
- [ ]
- [ ]
- [ ]
- [ ]
- [ ]
- [ ]
- [ ]
- [ ]

THIS OR THAT

My Cinema Style

THIS	THAT
○ home theater	○ movie theater
○ popcorn	○ candy
○ solo	○ with friends
○ matinee	○ evening
○ rom-com	○ horror
○ comedy	○ tearjerker
○ drama	○ action
○ fantasy	○ sci-fi
○ total darkness	○ mood lighting
○ couch	○ recliner
○ movie marathon	○ series binge
○ midnight premiere	○ opening weekend
○ silence	○ cheering
○ iced drink	○ hot drink
○ brand theater	○ indie theater
○ summer blockbuster	○ limited screening
○ dinner before	○ dinner during

VISUAL SCAVENGER

HUNT
— AT THE PARK —

PERSON FLYING A KITE	MAPLE LEAF	DOG PLAYING FETCH	OUTDOOR FITNESS CLASS
BIRD ON A STATUE	JOGGING STROLLER	FOOTBRIDGE	BOAT IN A POND OR LAKE
PERSON ON THE MONKEY BARS	PEOPLE PLAYING A GAME/ ORGANIZED SPORT	FOOD STAND	CLIMBING TREE
PERSON BAREFOOT IN THE GRASS	PICNIC	ELDERLY COUPLE ON A BENCH	NEON SHOES

SCRIBBLY
SKETCHES

**When boredom strikes, what
better way to muddle through it
than with sketching, doodling,
and creating!**

Whether you're anxious, stressed, or just plain bored, try this breath prayer and allow the truth of the words to wash over you and fill you with peace. For each breath, inhale through your nose for four to five seconds, and then exhale through your mouth for four to five seconds, all while meditating on the phrases below. Repeat five to seven times, or as much as needed.

(INHALE)

I am deeply loved

BREATH PRAYER

(EXHALE)

and capable of great love.

SHADING BY NUMBERS

1 2 3 4

HINT: Start with lighter shading. You can always go darker if you need to!

BOREDOM:

the desire for desires.

—LEO TOLSTOY

MULTIPLAYER GAMES

FOR THE MOMENTS WHEN YOU'RE BORED AND feeling social, try one of the activities in this section. Since they all require at least two people, grab a friend or family member to complete it with you. If you're out and about and up for an extra challenge, try making a new friend and inviting them to beat boredom with you!

JUST
FOR
LAUGHS

WHAT ARE THE STRONGEST DAYS?
Sundays and Saturdays; the rest are weekdays.

WHAT DID THE OCEAN SAY TO THE BEACH?
Nothing. It just waved.

WHAT'S THE BEST THING ABOUT SWITZERLAND?
I don't know, but the flag is a big plus!

HOW MANY EARS DOES SPOCK HAVE?
Three: the left ear, the right ear, and the final front-ear (frontier).

WHAT BRANCH OF THE MILITARY RECRUITS BABIES?
The infantry.

WHAT TEN-LETTER WORD STARTS WITH GAS?
Automobile.

WHAT KIND OF CHEF WILL BRING YOU TO COURT?
A sous (sue) chef.

DID YOU HEAR ABOUT THE MAN WHO EVAPORATED?
He will be missed (mist).

WHAT'S THE SCARIEST PLANT IN THE FOREST?
BamBOO.

WHAT DO ROBOTS DIP IN SALSA?
Microchips.

WHAT'S BLUE AND NOT VERY HEAVY?
Light blue.

WHAT DID CAPTAIN HOOK SAY ON THE MORNING OF HIS EIGHTIETH BIRTHDAY?
Aye, matey (I'm eighty).

WHAT DO YOU CALL A MONK THAT SELLS POTATO CHIPS?
Chip-monk.

TIC-TAC-TOE
CHAMPIONSHIPS

Grab a pencil and a buddy and gear up for some epic Tic-Tac-Toe Olympics. Use *X*'s, *O*'s, or any other symbols you like and see who can get three in a row first (horizontally, vertically, or diagonally). May the quickest mind win!

WINNER: _Kermit_

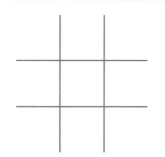

WINNER: _____

WINNER: _____

WINNER: _____

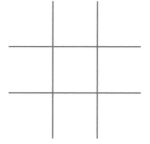

WINNER: _____

WINNER: _____

WINNER: _____

WINNER: _____

WINNER: _____

WINNER: _____

WINNER: _____

WINNER: _____

WINNER: _____

WINNER: _____

WINNER: _____

WINNER: _____

WINNER: _____

WINNER: _____

WINNER: _____

WINNER: _____

WINNER: _____

WINNER: _____

WINNER: _____

WINNER: _____

WINNER: _____

WINNER: _____

WINNER: _____

WINNER: _____

WINNER: _____

WINNER: _____

WINNER: _____

WINNER: _____

WINNER: _____

WINNER: _____

WINNER: _____

WINNER: _____

WINNER: _____

WINNER: _____

WINNER: _____

WINNER: _____

WINNER: _____

WINNER: _____

WINNER: _____

WINNER: _____

WINNER: _____

WINNER: _____

WINNER: _____

DOTS AND BOXES

Challenge one or more friends to a battle of wits, dots-and-boxes style. Taking turns, connect any two neighboring dots with a single straight line (horizontal or vertical only). Whenever your line "closes" a box, fill it with your first initial or another symbol of your choice and then go again. Once the grid is full of boxes, count them to see who has the most. May the best strategist win!

WINNER: _____Skywalker_____

WINNER: _____

107

WINNER: _____

WINNER: _____

WINNER: _____

WINNER: _____

WINNER: _____

WINNER: _____

WINNER: _____

WINNER: _____

WINNER: _____

WINNER: _____

DID YOU KNOW . . .

Swifts can fly for extremely long periods of time without ever needing to land. In fact, one study tracked a single swift's flight at ten months with only a two-hour cumulative break.[1]

Otters hold hands while they sleep so they don't float away from each other on the waves.[2]

Since guinea pigs are such social animals, it is illegal in Switzerland to own only one.[3]

The tongue of an average blue whale weighs about the same as an adult elephant.[4]

In Turin, Italy, pet owners must walk their dogs at least three times a day.[5]

Much like baby humans suck their thumbs, baby elephants will suck their trunks as a soothing mechanism.[6]

Crocodiles are all about being serious and are physically incapable of sticking their tongues out.[7]

Flying at a consistent rate of thirteen miles per hour, the grey-headed albatross can circumnavigate the globe in forty-six days.[8]

ABOUT ANIMALS?

HUMAN SCAVENGER

— SOMEONE WHO . . . —

HAS DRESSED IN COSPLAY	**HAS MADE YOU LAUGH**
HAS PAID IT FORWARD	**SPEAKS MORE THAN TWO LANGUAGES**
HAS BEEN ON TV	**HAS VISITED FOUR OR MORE CONTINENTS**
HAS MORE THAN FIVE SIBLINGS	**IS AN OCTOGENARIAN**

For this scavenger hunt, you'll need to get a little more creative and maybe even step outside your comfort zone. Instead of noticing things around you, try to find people who fit the following criteria. Ask friends, family members, or people you might be sitting next to on a plane or in a waiting room. On the blank line beneath each item, jot down where you "found" this person, or maybe get an autograph!

JUST CELEBRATED A BIRTHDAY
_____

IS DRINKING YOUR FAVORITE DRINK
_____

LOVES YOUR FAVORITE FANDOM
_____

HAS A "Z" IN THEIR NAME
_____

CAN DO A FLIP
_____

HAS AN UNUSUAL COLLECTION
_____

HAS LIVED IN ANOTHER COUNTRY
_____

KNOWS AT LEAST SIX DIGITS OF PI
_____

CONVERSATION STARTERS

Whether you're hanging out with friends or stranded somewhere with strangers, impress everyone around you with these clever conversation starters.

If you had to spend a million dollars in twenty-four hours, how would you spend it?

IF YOU COULD HAVE BRUNCH WITH ANYONE, ALIVE OR DEAD, WHO WOULD IT BE?

Which fictional family do you wish you could be part of?

WHAT IS ONE OF YOUR WEIRD SKILLS OR TALENTS?

If you could've witnessed anything in the Bible, what would you have wanted to see?

Which trip or vacation do you wish you could repeat?

What is the best meal you've had recently?

WHAT RECENT BOOK, MOVIE, OR PODCAST HAS HAD THE GREATEST EFFECT ON YOU?

IF YOU COULD START ANY NEW PROFESSION TOMORROW, WHICH WOULD YOU CHOOSE?

WHEN WAS THE LAST TIME YOU FELT TRULY RESTED?

What brings you the most joy?

WHAT HAS BEEN YOUR MOST MEMORABLE INTERACTION WITH A STRANGER?

If you could become an animal for a day, which would you want to be?

If you could tour anywhere in the world for a day, where would you go and whom would you choose as your tour guide?

Which character from television, literature, or a movie would you like to be best friends with?

IF YOU COULD HAVE A HOUSE ANYWHERE IN THE WORLD, WHERE WOULD IT BE?

What from your childhood do you wish would come back into popularity? What do you hope never comes back?

IF YOU COULD BECOME AN EXPERT AT ONE SKILL, WHAT WOULD IT BE?

Whether you're hanging out with friends or stranded somewhere with strangers, impress everyone around you with these clever conversation starters.

What was your favorite book as a child? Or what book did you reread over and over?

WHAT'S THE LAST MOVIE THAT MADE YOU CRY?

What's your favorite go-to tip, piece of advice, or book or movie suggestion to give other people?

Who is your biblical hero?

IF YOUR LIFE WERE MADE INTO A MOVIE, WHAT GENRE WOULD IT BE AND WHO WOULD PLAY YOU?

What is the next thing you want to accomplish?

What were your fifteen minutes of fame?

What three movies do you think the next generation should definitely watch?

WHAT IS ONE OF YOUR MOST VIVID MEMORIES?

If you could spend three months living anywhere in the world, where would that be?

Would you rather venture into deep space or the deep ocean? Why?

If your life were a TV show, what would your theme song be?

WHAT HOBBIES DID YOU HAVE AS A CHILD? WHAT HOBBIES DO YOU HAVE NOW?

Where's the strangest place you've fallen asleep?

WHAT IS YOUR FAVORITE HOLIDAY OR SEASON?

What's the most interesting fact that most people don't know about you?

WHO WAS YOUR FIRST CELEBRITY CRUSH?

WHAT IS YOUR EARLIEST MEMORY?

What random topic could you give a twenty-minute presentation on with no preparation?

Regardless of your current age, what do you want to be when you grow up?

SCRIPTURE MEMORY

PSALM 46

Have a few extra minutes? Read through this passage and see how much of it you can memorize.

God is our refuge and strength,
    an ever-present help in trouble.
Therefore we will not fear, though the
        earth give way
        and the mountains fall into the heart
        of the sea,
though its waters roar and foam
    and the mountains quake with their
        surging.

There is a river whose streams make
        glad the city of God,
    the holy place where the Most High
        dwells.
God is within her, she will not fall;
    God will help her at break of day.
Nations are in uproar, kingdoms fall;
    he lifts his voice, the earth melts.

The Lord Almighty is with us;
    the God of Jacob is our fortress.

Come and see what the Lord has done,
    the desolations he has brought on
        the earth.
He makes wars cease
    to the ends of the earth.
He breaks the bow and shatters the
        spear;
    he burns the shields with fire.
He says, "Be still, and know that I am
        God;
    I will be exalted among the nations,
    I will be exalted in the earth."

The Lord Almighty is with us;
    the God of Jacob is our fortress.

JUST
FOR
LAUGHS

Animal Edition

WHAT DID THE BUFFALO SAY TO HIS SON WHEN HE LEFT FOR SCHOOL?
Bison (Bye, son)!

WHY DO COWS WEAR BELLS?
Because their horns don't work.

EVER WONDER WHY WHEN GEESE FLY IN A *V*, ONE SIDE IS LONGER THAN THE OTHER?
Because one side has more geese.

WHAT DO YOU CALL A LAZY BABY KANGAROO?
A pouch potato.

WHAT SOUND DO PORCUPINES MAKE WHEN THEY KISS?
"Ouch!"

WHO DELIVERS CHRISTMAS PRESENTS TO CATS?
Santa Claws.

WHY DON'T CATS PLAY POKER IN THE WILD?
Too many cheetahs.

WHY DID THE PIG HAVE INK ALL OVER HIS FACE?
Because he just came out of the pen.

WHAT DO YOU CALL A GREAT DOG DETECTIVE?
Sherlock Bones.

WHERE DID THE SHEEP GO ON VACATION?
The Baaaahamas.

WHAT'S GRAY, HAS BIG EARS, AND HAS A GIANT TRUNK?
A mouse going on vacation.

WHY DID THE ALLIGATOR CROSS THE ROAD?
Because it wanted to be bayou (by you).

WHY HAVE CHICKENS STOPPED CROSSING THE ROAD?
They now call an "ewe"ber.

STORY
BOREDS

Time to practice those writing skills! Come up with a hilarious story with your friends, or get out of your comfort zone and ask people in your bus, your office, a coffee shop, a park, or another location to suggest words for you. However your story ends up, it's sure to be a bestseller!

THE LAST TIME I WAS BORED

Have I got a story for you. The other day, I was at _____
(place)

and feeling really bored. So I decided to _____ . That
(verb)

kept me busy for about _____ minutes, but then I got bored
(number)

again, so I called _____ and told them to meet me
(friend's name)

at _____ . When we arrived, the place was _____ ,
(another place)   (adjective)

and everyone there was _____ . One guy was even
(-ing verb)

_____ , but it wasn't until I saw the _____ on
(another -ing verb)   (noun, plural)

the _____ that I had an idea. To _____
(type of furniture)   (verb)

boredom, we could try _____ .
(activity)

To do that, the first thing we needed was a(n) _____
(noun)

from the local _____ . Unfortunately, we
(type of store)

couldn't find one, but my friend had a(n) _____ ,
(another noun)

which worked just the same. With that in hand, we went to

_____ and started _____ .
     (place)   (-ing verb)

A(n) _____ passed by us, said _____ ,
     (type of person)   (exclamation)

and then joined us. After that, _____ more people joined,
                          (number)

and soon we had a whole _____ going.
                          (type of gathering)

And then, as if that weren't _____ enough, a(n)
                             (adjective)

_____ showed up and started live streaming us.
(another type of person)

The next thing you know, we had _____ views and were
                             (number)

going viral on _____ . "Crowd _____ the
          (type of social media)   (present-tense verb)

World with _____ Stunt" read the headline. The post
         (adjective)

even got reshared by _____ . Who knew I would
                 (name of celebrity)

get _____ _____ of fame just because I was bored!
   (number)   (measurement of time)

STORY
BOREDS

Time to practice those writing skills! Come up with a hilarious story with your friends, or get out of your comfort zone and ask people in your bus, your office, a coffee shop, a park, or another location to suggest words for you. However your story ends up, it's sure to be a bestseller!

A FANTASY ADVENTURE

From the journals of _____ , the _____ ,
(person's name)   (type of fantasy creature)

in the year _____ .
(number)

It was a(n) _____ morning _____ _____
(adjective)   (number)   (measurement of time, plural)

ago, when I finally embarked on the quest for the _____ .
(noun)

Before the sun was up, I packed my satchel with _____
(food, plural)

and set out on the journey with my closest companion,

_____ , a(n) _____ who knows how to
(pet name)   (animal)

_____ , which I knew would come in handy.
(verb)

We soon entered the Forest of _____ , a(n) _____
(noun)   (adjective)

place supposedly home to hundreds of _____ .
(type of creature or animal, plural)

Thankfully, we didn't come across any and were able to

124

_____ reach the Bridge of _____ . As I
  (-ly adverb)   (noun, plural)

expected, the wizard of _____ was standing
                        (something found in nature, plural)

on it, and he asked me, "_____ ?"
                                (question)

I told him I didn't know but that I would give him a(n)

_____ if he let me pass. He paused for _____
  (object)   (number)

seconds, but then he agreed.

After the bridge, we _____ for _____
                     (past-tense verb)   (number)

_____ before coming to the Lake of _____ .
  (length of distance, plural)   (noun)

There we met a(n) _____ , who told
                (type of fantasy creature)

us she would grant one wish. I explained that we were on a

quest, and she revealed that we would find what we were

seeking in the nearby Cave of _____ . We followed
                            (noun, plural)

her directions, but when we came to the cave, we found

a(n) _____ _____
     (type of fantasy creature)   (-ing verb)

in front of it. We had to _____ to get past
                        (verb)

him, but _____ caused a distraction by
         (same pet name)

_____ at him, and I was able to slip inside. It was
  (-ing verb)

then that I discovered the _____ _____
                     (adjective)   (noun)

of _____ . . .
   (fantasy name)

STORY BORFDS

Time to practice those writing skills! Come up with a hilarious story with your friends, or get out of your comfort zone and ask people in your bus, your office, a coffee shop, a park, or another location to suggest words for you. However your story ends up, it's sure to be a bestseller!

AN AVERAGE DAY IN MY LIFE

Today, I woke up at my usual time of _____ and grabbed my
                                    (time)

_____ off my bedside table. After throwing on my
        (object)

favorite _____ , I headed to the kitchen for a(n)
          (item of clothing)

_____ cup of _____ and some _____ .
   (adjective)   (type of beverage)   (type of food, plural)

While I ate, I _____ , as I often do. After breakfast,
                (past-tense activity)

I finished getting ready for the day by _____ my teeth
                                          (-ing verb)

and _____ the rest of my clothes. Then I packed up my
      (-ing verb)

_____ and my _____ and headed to work.
   (object)   (another type of food)

I took a(n) _____ as usual and arrived at the office
             (mode of transportation)

right on time. After greeting the _____ ,
                                              (type of person)

I rode the elevator with _____ other people up to the
                          (number)

_____ floor, where I _____
(ordinal number: 1st, 2nd, 3rd, etc.)   (verb)

meetings, _____ clients, and _____ projects
                 (verb)   (verb)
every day. All of that is very _____ work for my
                                      (adjective)
company, _____ _____ , which
              (adjective)   (noun)
is famous for_____ and has been called the
                     (-ing verb)
_____ in the industry.
  (superlative adjective)

As usual, the office was _____ and the workday
                                 (adjective)
passed by _____ . As soon as it was over, I went to
            (-ly adverb)
the gym, where I _____ and lifted _____-pound
                    (past-tense verb)   (number)
weights. Then I met some friends at a(n) _____ for
                                               (location)
happy hour. As usual, we had a(n) _____ time. Later,
                                         (adjective)
I went back home and ate _____ for dinner
                              (another type of food)
while watching _____ , which is one
                     (TV show or movie title)
of my favorites. Then I took a(n) _____ shower and got
                                       (adjective)
ready for bed. Before falling asleep, I read _____ pages of
                                                (number)
my favorite book, _____ . Then it was lights out.
                      (book title)
Just another _____ day!
                 (adjective)

Time to practice those writing skills! Come up with a hilarious story with your friends, or get out of your comfort zone and ask people in your bus, your office, a coffee shop, a park, or another location to suggest words for you. However your story ends up, it's sure to be a bestseller!

MY BESTSELLING NOVEL

Once upon a time, there was a _____ who lived
                                   (type of person/occupation)

in a(n) _____. She was known for _____
         (type of building)   (-ing verb)

the best _____ , and people would often travel _____
          (noun, plural)   (number)

miles to buy her work. But for all her fame, she had only a(n)

_____ for a friend, and she was often _____ .
   (animal)   (negative adjective)

One day, a(n) _____ visited the city and announced
                (type of person/occupation)

a competition. He promised to award a(n) _____ to the
                                           (object)

person who could create the _____ _____ .
                              (superlative adjective)   (noun)

The girl _____ signed up and spent the next several
           (-ly adverb)

_____ preparing her masterpiece. _____
(measurement of time, plural)   (adjective)

judges occasionally checked in on the contestants' work and

promoted the best ones to the next round. Soon the girl found

herself in the final round against a(n) _____ _____
(adjective) type of person/occupation

and a(n) _____ _____ . Three finalists, but
(adjective) type of person/occupation

only one could win the prize.

While she was in the _____ working on her project, one
(generic location)

of the other contestants—whose name was _____—
(male name)

joined her. Speaking _____ , he told her that the other
(-ly adverb)

contestant was cheating by _____ . Just then, they both
(-ing verb)

noticed the third contestant _____ nearby. That was
(-ing verb)

when the girl knew _____ was right. He asked
(same male name)

if they should turn her in, but the girl had another idea. "Let's

team up and _____ her at her own game."
(verb)

So they did. At the final judging, their combined piece was so

_____ that even _____ offered _____ dollars
(adjective) (celebrity name) (number)

to buy it. With the prize and their sudden earnings, the two

winners _____ each other and decided to _____ .
(past-tense verb) (verb)

After that, they went into business together to create the finest

_____ the world had ever seen. And they lived
(noun, plural)

_____ ever after.
(-ly adverb)

Time to practice those writing skills! Come up with a hilarious story with your friends, or get out of your comfort zone and ask people in your bus, your office, a coffee shop, a park, or another location to suggest words for you. However your story ends up, it's sure to be a bestseller!

THE TRIP OF A LIFETIME

The day is finally here! After _____ of waiting,
(measurement of time, plural)

you're off to visit _____ , home to the world's only
(city in the world)

_____ and the largest number of _____ .
(landmark)   (animal, plural)

You've packed your passport, _____ , _____ ,
(item of clothing)   (snack)

and your favorite _____ . And now you're ready to
(noun)

go catch that _____ , which will take you
(mode of transportation)

_____ to your destination. You're planning to arrive at
(-ly adverb)

_____ , when you'll check in to your _____ and
(time)   (type of building)

organize your vacation itinerary.

First on the list is visiting the city's _____ and trying
(second landmark)

the local _____ . Then you'll grab your _____
(type of food)   (item of clothing)

and head for the _____ . When you finish there, you'll
(place)

meet up with _____ and go tour the museum
                (friend's name)

downtown, which houses _____ _____ and
                        (number)   (noun, plural)

a _____ signed by _____ . After that,
    (noun)   (celebrity name)

you'll have _____ for dinner and then go _____ .
            (type of food)   (-ing verb)

At last, you'll take a _____ back to your
                        (mode of transportation)

_____ and take a(n) _____ shower. Then
(repeat type of building)   (adjective)

you'd better get _____ hours of sleep, since this _____
                 (number)   (adjective)

vacation will last another _____ _____ !
                           (number) (measurement of time, plural)

JUST
FOR
LAUGHS

Bible Edition

WHY COULDN'T THEY PLAY CARDS ON THE ARK?
Noah was always standing on the deck.

WHO WAS THE SHORTEST MAN IN THE BIBLE?
Nehemiah (Knee-high-miah) or Bildad the Shuhite (Shoe-height).

WHAT U.S. STATE IS MENTIONED IN THE BIBLE?
Arkansas (Noah looked out of the ark-and-saw . . .).

WHY IS MOSES CONSIDERED THE MOST REBELLIOUS PERSON IN HISTORY?
He broke all Ten Commandments at once.

WHERE IS SOLOMON'S TEMPLE LOCATED?
On the side of his head.

DID YOU KNOW THERE WAS TENNIS IN THE BIBLE?
It says that David played in Saul's court.

WHO WAS THE SMALLEST MAN IN THE BIBLE?
Peter, because he slept on his watch.

WHERE IS THE FIRST BASEBALL GAME IN THE BIBLE?
In the beginning (big inning). Eve stole first; Adam stole second.

WHAT KIND OF MAN WAS BOAZ BEFORE HE GOT MARRIED?
Ruth-less.

PASSING NOTES

Fancy a friendly chat? Use the following pages to strike up a conversation, sans talking. Instead of passing individual pages (no tearing, please!), pass the book. Invite one or more friends to join. (Not recommended for use in classrooms or conference rooms.)

136

Have a few extra
minutes? Read
through this
passage and see
how much of it you
can memorize.

Answer me quickly, LORD;
    my spirit fails.
Do not hide your face from me
    or I will be like those who go
        down to the pit.
Let the morning bring me word
    of your unfailing love,
    for I have put my trust in you.
Show me the way I should go,
    for to you I entrust my life.
Rescue me from my enemies,
        LORD,
    for I hide myself in you.
Teach me to do your will,
    for you are my God;
may your good Spirit
    lead me on level ground.

For your name's sake, LORD,
    preserve my life;
    in your righteousness, bring
        me out of trouble.
In your unfailing love, silence
    my enemies;
    destroy all my foes,
    for I am your servant.

PLEASE

LEARN   THE   LINGO

I'M SORRY

AFRIKAANS – Asseblief	**AFRIKAANS** – Ek is jammer
ARABIC – من فضلك [Min faḍlik]	**ARABIC** – أنا آسف. [Anā ʾāsef]
DUTCH – Alsjeblieft	**DUTCH** – Sorry
ENGLISH – Please	**ENGLISH** – I'm sorry
FRENCH – S'il vous plaît (plural)	**FRENCH** – Je suis désolé
GERMAN – Bitte	**GERMAN** – Es tut mir leid / Entschuldigung
HAWAIIAN – E ʻoluʻolu ʻoe	**HAWAIIAN** – E kala mai i aʻu
HINDI – कृपया [Krpaya]	**HINDI** – मैं माफ़ी चाहता हूँ / चाहती हूँ [main maafii caahaTaa huun / caahaTii huun]
ITALIAN – Per favore	**ITALIAN** – Mi dispiace / Spiacente
JAPANESE – お願いします [Onegaishimasu]	**JAPANESE** – ごめんなさい [Gomen nasai]
MANDARIN – 请 [Qǐng]	**MANDARIN** – 对不起 [Duì bù qǐ]
PORTUGUESE – Por favor	**PORTUGUESE** – Desculpa / Desculpe
RUSSIAN – Пожалуйста [Pahzhalsta]	**RUSSIAN** – Извините [Izvinite]
SPANISH – Por favor	**SPANISH** – Lo siento
SWAHILI – Tafadhali	**SWAHILI** – Samahani
UKRAINIAN – будь ласка [Bud' laska]	**UKRAINIAN** – Вибач [Vybach]

BORED BUDDY TOURNAMENT

Think you're a wordsmith? Come up with the trickiest word you know and see if anyone can guess it before you draw your entire bored buddy! (Similar to hangman, if you're familiar with that game, but a bored buddy is much friendlier to draw!)

WRONG LETTERS

J Z P M A
L I C T K

B O R E _

WRONG LETTERS

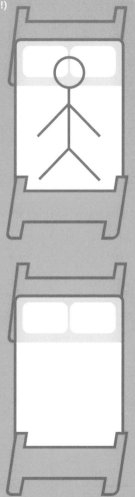

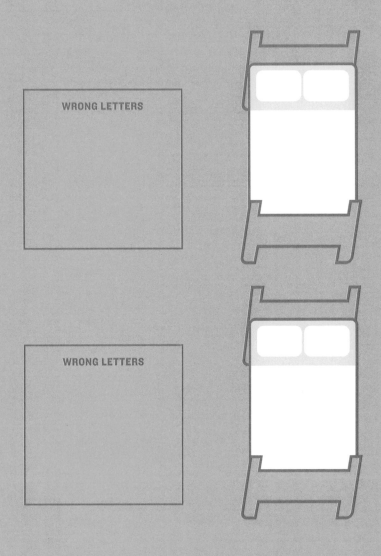

WRONG LETTERS

WRONG LETTERS

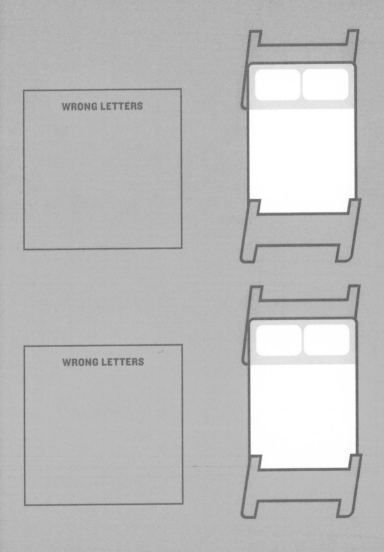

WRONG LETTERS

WRONG LETTERS

145

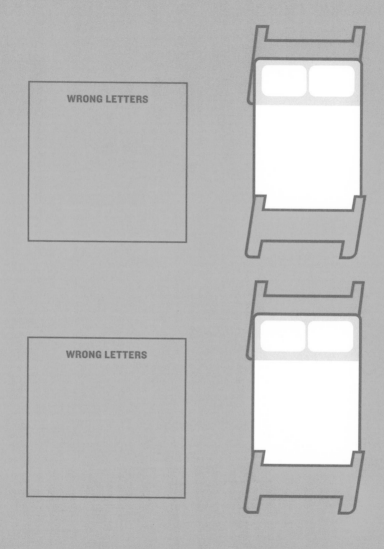

WRONG LETTERS

WRONG LETTERS

WRONG LETTERS

WRONG LETTERS

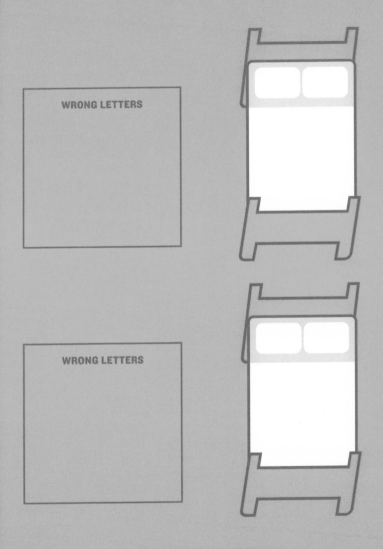

147

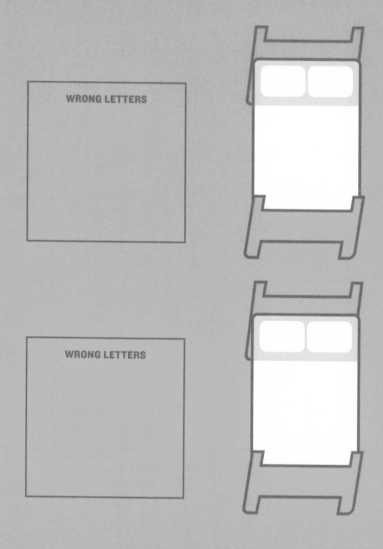

WRONG LETTERS

WRONG LETTERS

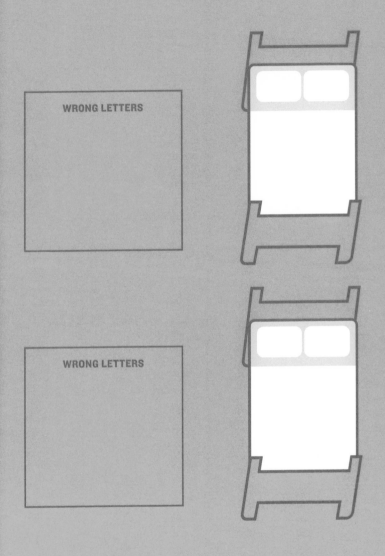

WRONG LETTERS

WRONG LETTERS

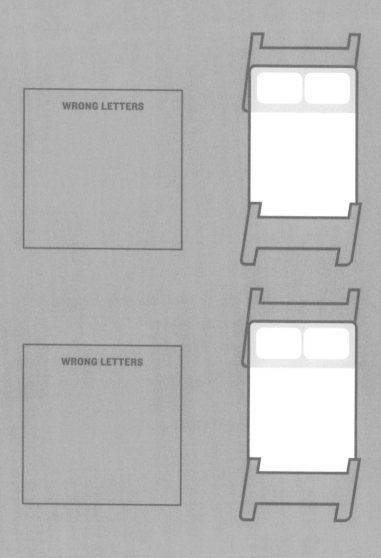

WRONG LETTERS

WRONG LETTERS

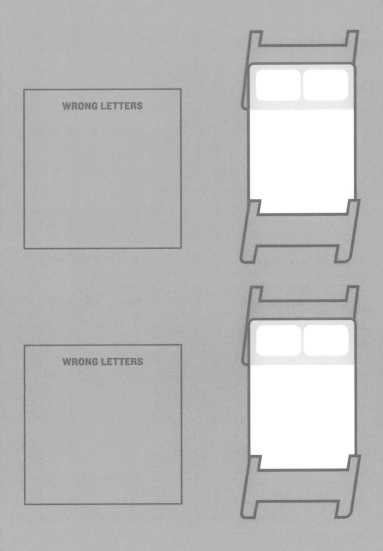

WRONG LETTERS

WRONG LETTERS

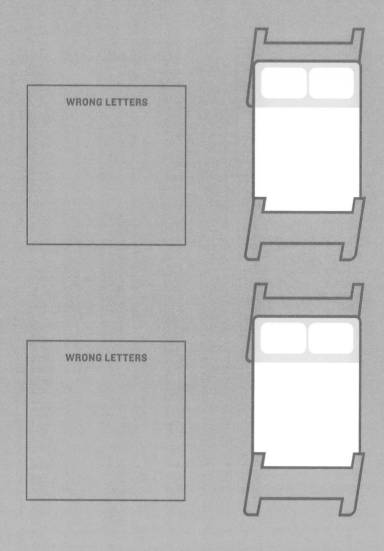

WRONG LETTERS

WRONG LETTERS

JUST
FOR
LAUGHS

Sports Edition

WHY IS CINDERELLA SO BAD AT SOCCER?
She always runs away from the ball!

WHY ARE BASKETBALL PLAYERS MESSY EATERS?
Because they are always dribbling!

HOW IS A BASEBALL TEAM SIMILAR TO A PANCAKE?
They both need a good batter.

WHY ARE BASEBALL GAMES AT NIGHT?
The bats sleep during the day.

WHY DID THE GOLFER WEAR TWO PAIRS OF PANTS?
In case he got a hole in one!

WHY CAN'T YOU PLAY SOCCER WITH PIGS?
They hog the ball.

HOW DO WE KNOW THAT SOCCER REFEREES ARE HAPPY?
Because they whistle while they work.

DID YOU HEAR THE JOKE ABOUT THE POP FLY?
Forget it. It's way over your head.

WHAT DO YOU GET WHEN YOU MIX A BOXER AND A VOLLEYBALL PLAYER?
Spiked punch.

"I'm bored."

"Hi, Bored. I'm Mom."

—ALL MOMS EVERYWHERE

ADVENTURES IN BEATING BOREDOM

TWO THINGS ARE CERTAIN IN LIFE: death and boredom. But boredom doesn't have to trouble us. After all, how we become bored is less important than what we do to overcome it.

Jokes aside, everyone's boredom journey is unique. Use the following pages to catalog your own adventures in recognizing when you're most likely to succumb to boredom and how you're learning to beat it.

MY BOREDOM LOG

Charting My Boredom Patterns

Date:

Time:

Location:

Reason for Boredom:

What Fixed the Boredom:

What I Learned About Myself:

Date:

Time:

Location:

Reason for Boredom:

What Fixed the Boredom:

What I Learned About Myself:

Date:

Time:

Location:

Reason for Boredom:

What Fixed the Boredom:

What I Learned About Myself:

Date:

Time:

Location:

Reason for Boredom:

What Fixed the Boredom:

What I Learned About Myself:

Date:

Time:

Location:

Reason for Boredom:

What Fixed the Boredom:

What I Learned About Myself:

Date:

Time:

Location:

Reason for Boredom:

What Fixed the Boredom:

What I Learned About Myself:

Date:

Time:

Location:

Reason for Boredom:

What Fixed the Boredom:

What I Learned About Myself:

Date: _____

Time: _____

Location: _____

Reason for Boredom: _____

What Fixed the Boredom: _____

What I Learned About Myself: _____

Date: _____

Time: _____

Location: _____

Reason for Boredom: _____

What Fixed the Boredom: _____

What I Learned About Myself: _____

Date: _____

Time: _____

Location: _____

Reason for Boredom: _____

What Fixed the Boredom: _____

What I Learned About Myself: _____

Date: _____

Time: _____

Location: _____

Reason for Boredom: _____

What Fixed the Boredom: _____

What I Learned About Myself: _____

Date:

Time:

Location:

Reason for Boredom:

What Fixed the Boredom:

What I Learned About Myself:

Date:

Time:

Location:

Reason for Boredom:

What Fixed the Boredom:

What I Learned About Myself:

Date:

Time:

Location:

Reason for Boredom:

What Fixed the Boredom:

What I Learned About Myself:

Date:

Time:

Location:

Reason for Boredom:

What Fixed the Boredom:

What I Learned About Myself:

Date: _____

Time: _____

Location: _____

Reason for Boredom: _____

What Fixed the Boredom: _____

What I Learned About Myself: _____

Date: _____

Time: _____

Location: _____

Reason for Boredom: _____

What Fixed the Boredom: _____

What I Learned About Myself: _____

Date: _____

Time: _____

Location: _____

Reason for Boredom: _____

What Fixed the Boredom: _____

What I Learned About Myself: _____

Date: _____

Time: _____

Location: _____

Reason for Boredom: _____

What Fixed the Boredom: _____

What I Learned About Myself: _____

Date:

Time:

Location:

Reason for Boredom:

What Fixed the Boredom:

What I Learned About Myself:

Date:

Time:

Location:

Reason for Boredom:

What Fixed the Boredom:

What I Learned About Myself:

Date:

Time:

Location:

Reason for Boredom:

What Fixed the Boredom:

What I Learned About Myself:

Date:

Time:

Location:

Reason for Boredom:

What Fixed the Boredom:

What I Learned About Myself:

WINS
AGAINST
BOREDOM

Capturing the Moments When I Beat Boredom

DATE OF BOREDOM	REASON FOR BOREDOM	I BROKE THE BOREDOM WITH THIS . . .	INSTEAD OF THIS . . .	BOREDOM SCORE
9/12	Put on hold	Scrolling Instagram	Watering my plants	2
9/15	Nothing to do	Reading a book	Staring at the ceiling	8

DATE OF BOREDOM	REASON FOR BOREDOM	I BROKE THE BOREDOM WITH THIS . . .	INSTEAD OF THIS . . .	BOREDOM SCORE

DATE OF BOREDOM	REASON FOR BOREDOM	I BROKE THE BOREDOM WITH THIS . . .	INSTEAD OF THIS . . .	BOREDOM SCORE

DATE OF BOREDOM	REASON FOR BOREDOM	I BROKE THE BOREDOM WITH THIS ...	INSTEAD OF THIS ...	BOREDOM SCORE

DATE OF BOREDOM	REASON FOR BOREDOM	I BROKE THE BOREDOM WITH THIS . . .	INSTEAD OF THIS . . .	BOREDOM SCORE

DATE OF BOREDOM	REASON FOR BOREDOM	I BROKE THE BOREDOM WITH THIS . . .	INSTEAD OF THIS . . .	BOREDOM SCORE

BOREDOM GOALS

Bucket List for When I'm Bored

Are you tired of boring moments taking the most out of you instead of you making the most of them? Why not create a "boredom bucket list" so you're prepared in advance the next time boredom strikes. We've included some ideas to help you get started:

- ☐ Learn how to say "thank you" in a new language

- ☐ Text a friend or family member you haven't talked to in a while

- ☐ Practice your autograph

- ☐ Start a to-read or to-watch list

- ☐ Delete files, emails, or photos you no longer need

- ☐ Look up a new recipe to try

- ☐ Pray for the people around you

- ☐ Think of a unique trait you like about yourself

- ☐ Do a two-minute workout

- ☐ Make a to-do list

- ☐ Memorize a Bible verse

- ☐ Say hello to someone you don't know

- ☐ Write your own riddle

- [ ] Look for something beautiful

- [ ] Think of one thing you're grateful for

- [ ] Do one activity in *The Bored Book*

- [ ]

- [ ]

- [ ]

- [ ]

- [ ]

- [ ]

- [ ]

- [ ]

- [ ]

- [ ]

- [ ]

- [ ]

- [ ]

- [ ]

WORD SEARCH ANSWER KEY

BORED WORD SEARCH ANSWER KEY

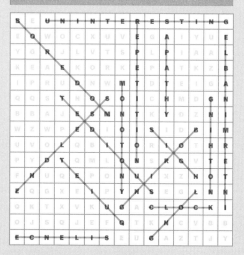

THOUGHTFUL WORD SEARCH ANSWER KEY

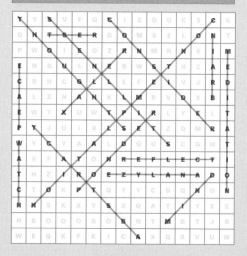

MINDFUL WORD SEARCH ANSWER KEY

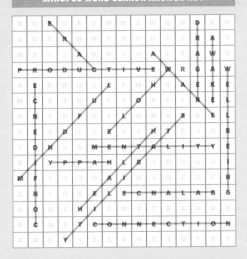

CREATIVE WORD SEARCH ANSWER KEY

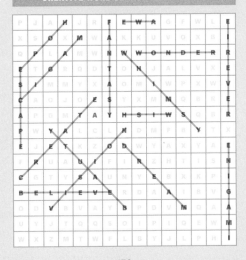

SOURCES

While we do possess a lot of random and useless knowledge, we'd like to credit the following sites for contributing some of the more interesting facts in this book:

www.beano.com/posts/weird-history-facts

www.bestlifeonline.com/fast-facts

www.boredpanda.com/interesting-food-facts

www.discovercorps.com/blog/40-crazy-travel-facts

www.explorethearchive.com/weird-history-facts

www.factanimal.com/animal-facts

www.lonelyplanet.com/articles/amazing-facts-about-travel

www.parade.com/1099930/marynliles/history-facts

www.thefactsite.com/top-100-random-funny-facts

www.thelawyerportal.com/blog/top-10-weirdest-laws-around-world

www.thepetexpress.co.uk/blog/general-interest/7-weird-animal-facts-that-you-didnt-know

www.weareteachers.com/fun-food-facts

Word searches made with the help of www.puzzlemaker.discoveryeducation.com.

NOTES

How Not to Be Bored

1. Carla Cantor, "Why Being Bored Can Be Hazardous to Your Health," *Columbia News*, November 8, 2019, https://news.columbia.edu/news/why-being-bored-can-be-hazardous -your-health.
2. Ashok Seshadri, "Boost Your Brain with Boredom," Mayo Clinic Health System, September 14, 2022, www.mayoclinichealthsystem.org/hometown-health/speaking-of-health/ boost-your-brain-with-boredom.
3. Max Knoblauch, "This Is How Often Americans Spend Their Lives Being Bored," *New York Post*, January 29, 2019, https://nypost.com/2019/01/29/this-is-how-often-americans-spend -their-lives-being-bored.
4. Ash Turner, "How Many Smartphones Are in the World?" BankMyCell, accessed April 13, 2023, www.bankmycell.com/blog/how-many-phones-are-in-the-world.

5. Lorena Castillo, "Technology Addiction Statistics [Fresh Research]," Gitnux, updated December 16, 2023, https://blog.gitnux.com/technology-addiction-statistics.

6. "Mental Health," World Health Organization, accessed April 14, 2023, www.who.int/health -topics/mental-health#tab=tab_2.

7. Knoblauch, "This Is How Often."

Solo Activities

1. Luke Ward, "100 Fun Facts That You'll Love to Know," The Fact Site, updated November 21, 2023, www.thefactsite.com/top-100-random-funny-facts.

2. Alex Daniel, "35 Fascinating Fast Facts for When You're Bored," BestLife, May 4, 2020, https:// bestlifeonline.com/fast-facts.

3. Maryn Liles, "125 Mind-Blowing Historic Facts & Trivia That Are Almost Too Weird to Be True," *Parade*, February 3, 2023, https://parade.com/1099930/marynliles/history-facts.

4. Daniel, "35 Fascinating Fast Facts."

5. Ward, "100 Fun Facts."

6. "About Harriet," Harriet Tubman Museum & Educational Center, www.harriettubmanmuseum center.org/about-harriet.

7. Ward, "100 Fun Facts."

8. "How Peanut Butter Met Jelly: Valentine's Day Edition," National Peanut Board, September 1, 2023, https://nationalpeanutboard.org/news/how-peanut-butter-met-jelly-valentines-day -edition.

9. Lorcan Fearon, "20 Weird Food Facts You Probably Didn't Know," Bored Panda, May 2, 2018, www.boredpanda.com/interesting-food-facts-lorcan-fearon.

10. Nikki Katz, "100+ Fascinating and Gross Food Facts for Kids," We Are Teachers, January 13, 2023, www.weareteachers.com/fun-food-facts.

11. Brianna Elliott, "19 Water-Rich Foods That Help You Stay Hydrated," Healthline, February 7, 2023, www.healthline.com/nutrition/19-hydrating-foods.

12. Kelsey Christine McConnell, "10 Weird History Facts That Will Change Your Perspective," The Archive, September 14, 2022, https://explorethearchive.com/weird-history-facts.

13. "15 Honey Facts Worth Buzzing About," Mental Floss, September 15, 2015, www.mentalfloss .com/article/68528/15-honey-facts-worth-buzzing-about.

14. Jack Palfrey, "25 Surprising Travel Facts That'll Make You See the World in a Whole New Light," Lonely Planet, April 2, 2020, www.lonelyplanet.com/articles/amazing-facts-about-travel.

15. Scott Dye, "40 Crazy Travel Facts," Discover Corps, November 12, 2018, https://discovercorps .com/blog/40-crazy-travel-facts.

16. Dye, "40 Crazy Travel Facts."

17. Palfrey, "25 Surprising Travel Facts."

18. Palfrey, "25 Surprising Travel Facts."

19. Ward, "100 Fun Facts."
20. Palfrey, "25 Surprising Travel Facts."
21. Dye, "40 Crazy Travel Facts."

Multiplayer Games

1. "The 101 Greatest Animal Facts," Fact Animal, accessed March 19, 2024, https://factanimal.com/animal-facts.
2. Luke Ward, "100 Fun Facts That You'll Love to Know," The Fact Site, updated November 21, 2023, www.thefactsite.com/top-100-random-funny-facts.
3. Ward, "100 Fun Facts."
4. "7 Weird Animal Facts That You Didn't Know," The Pet Express, accessed March 19, 2024, www.thepetexpress.co.uk/blog/general-interest/7-weird-animal-facts-that-you-didnt-know.
5. "10 Weird Laws from Around the World," The Lawyer Portal, March 13, 2023, www.thelawyerportal.com/blog/top-10-weirdest-laws-around-world.
6. "101 Greatest Animal Facts."
7. "Crocodilian," San Diego Zoo Wildlife Alliance, accessed February 21, 2024, https://animals.sandiegozoo.org/animals/crocodilian.
8. "101 Greatest Animal Facts."